About DICKHEAD

Outstanding Swear Word To Color For Stress Releasing

Ja Millie Hawthorn

I0463622

Happy Coloring!

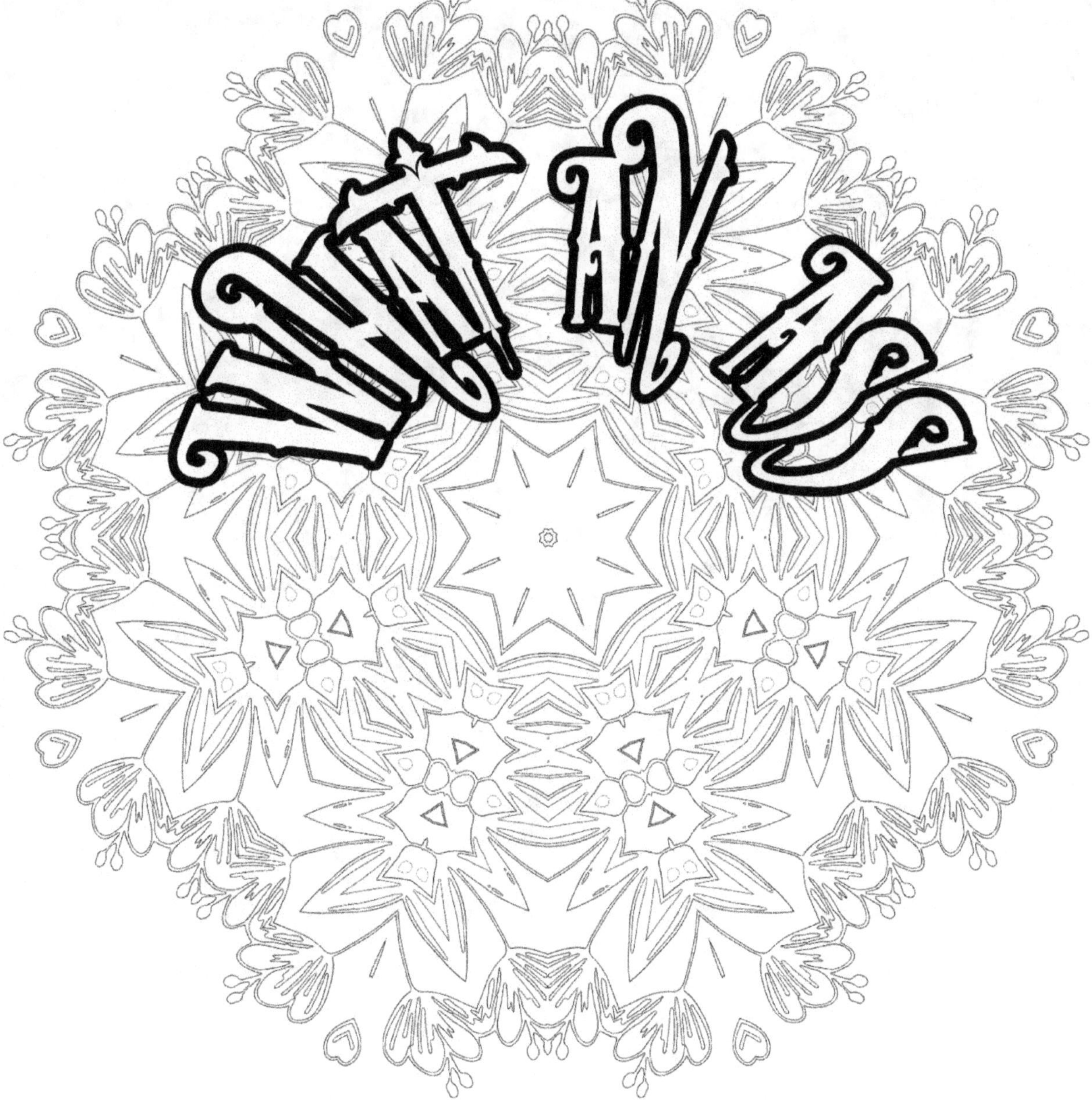
WHAT AN ASS

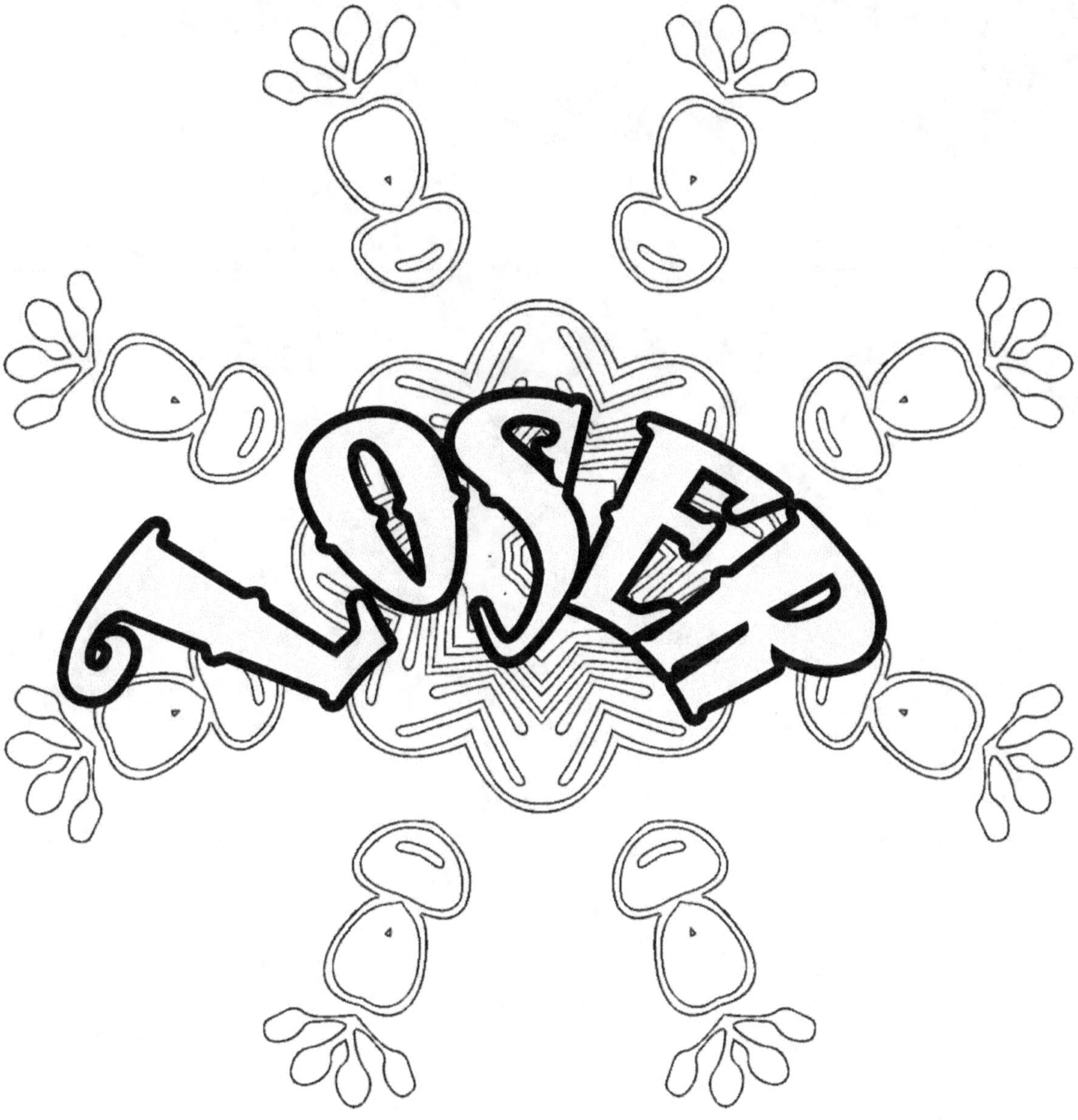
LOSER

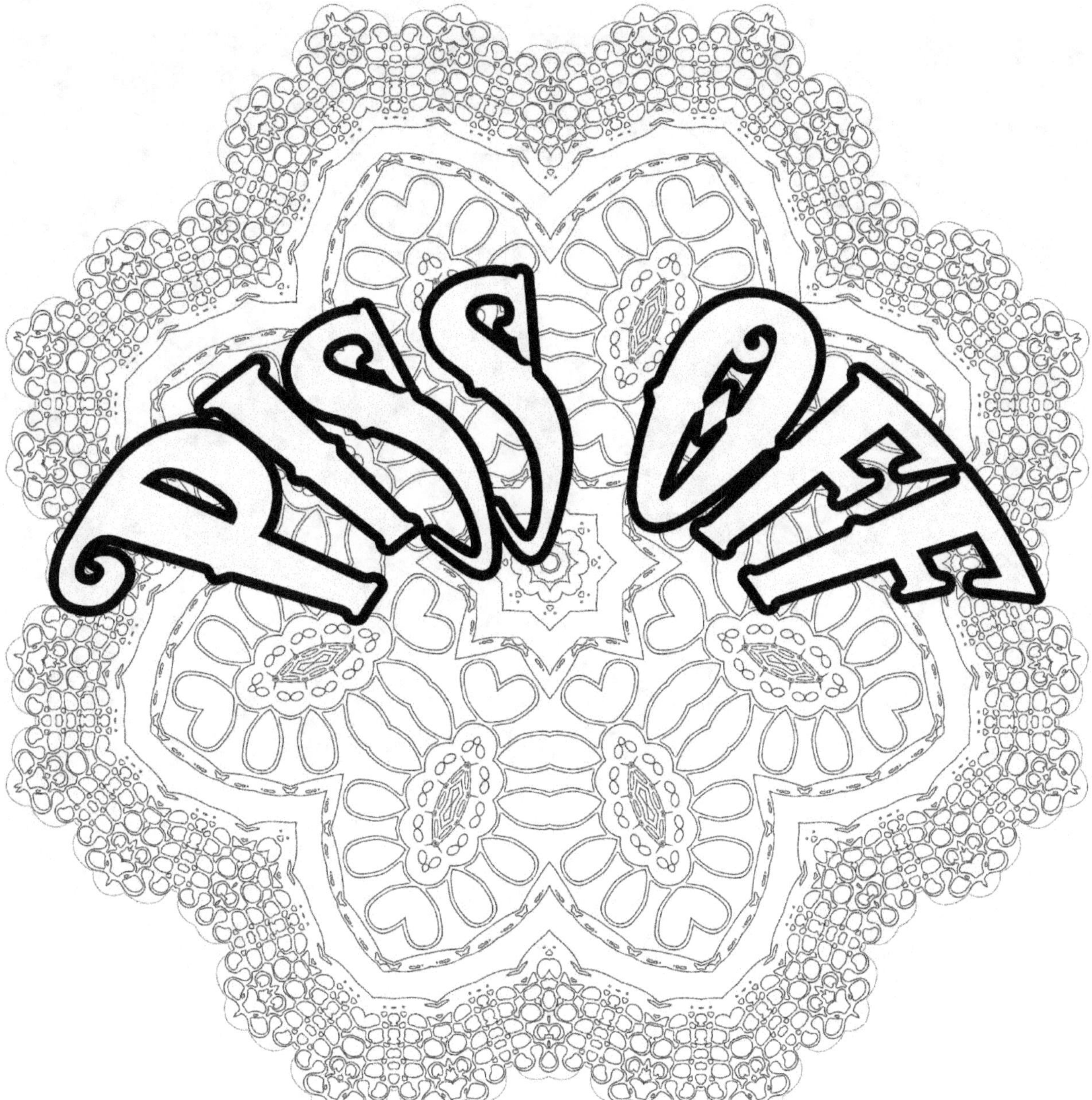
PISS OFF

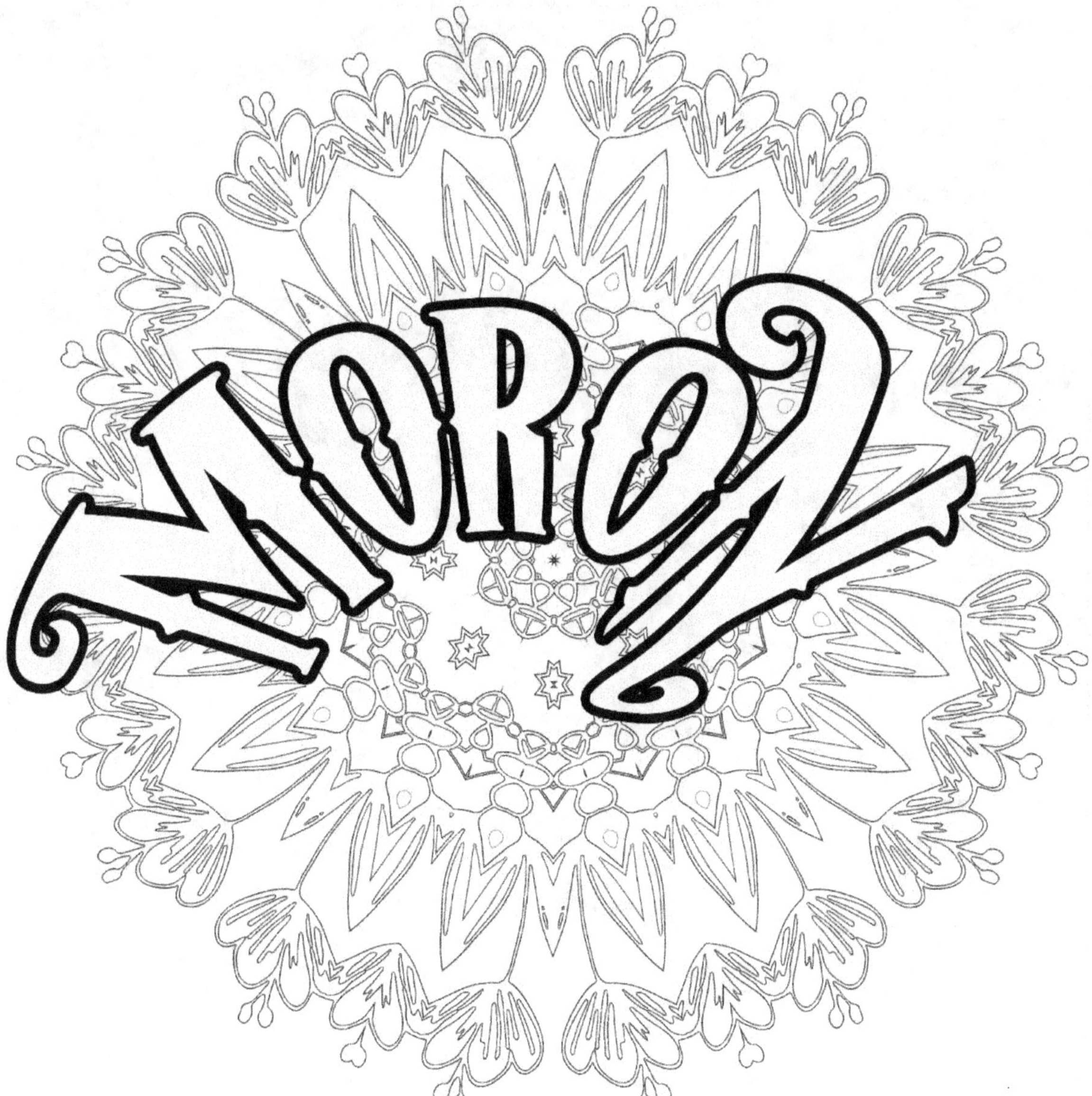
MORON

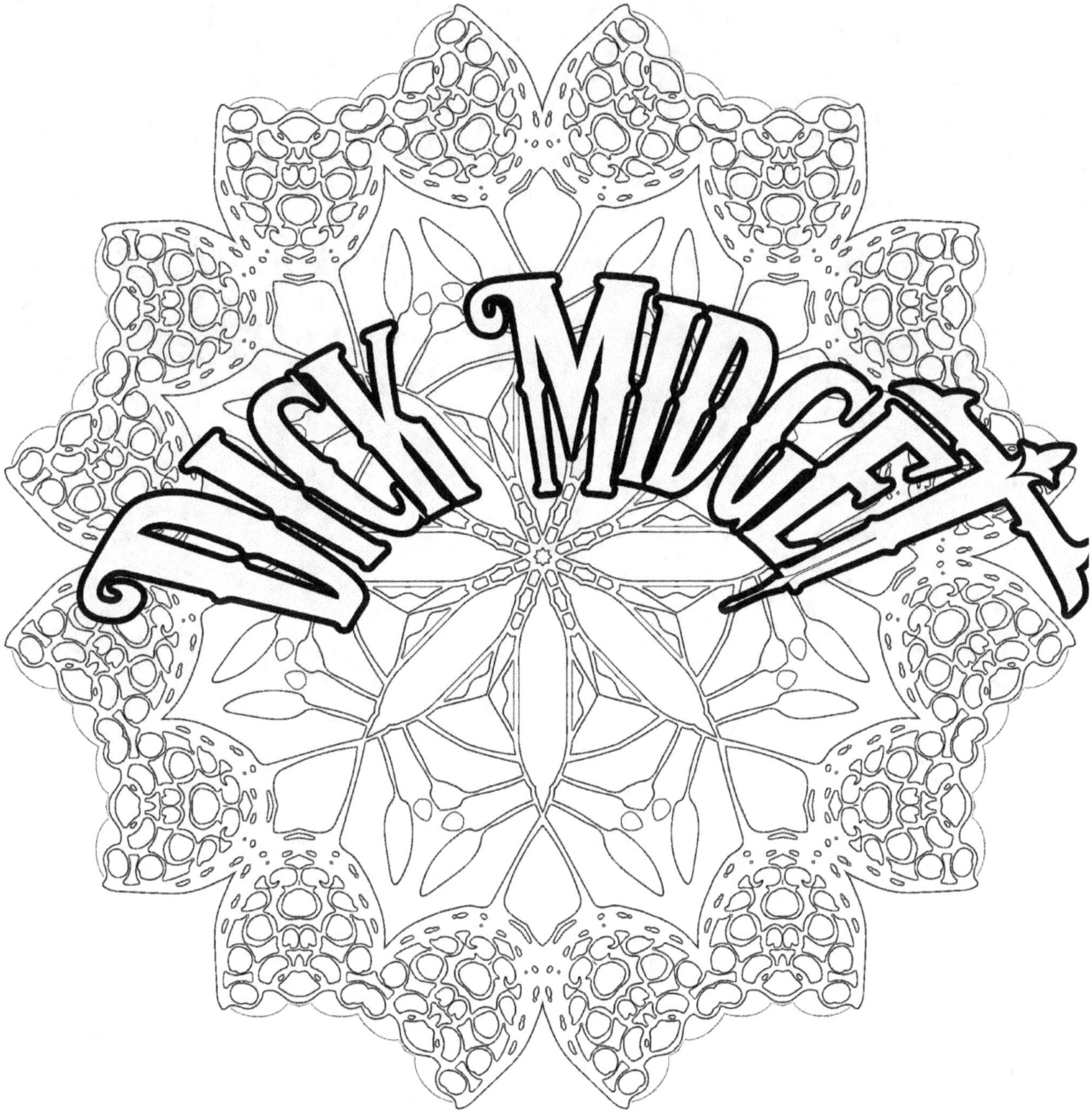
DICK MIDGET

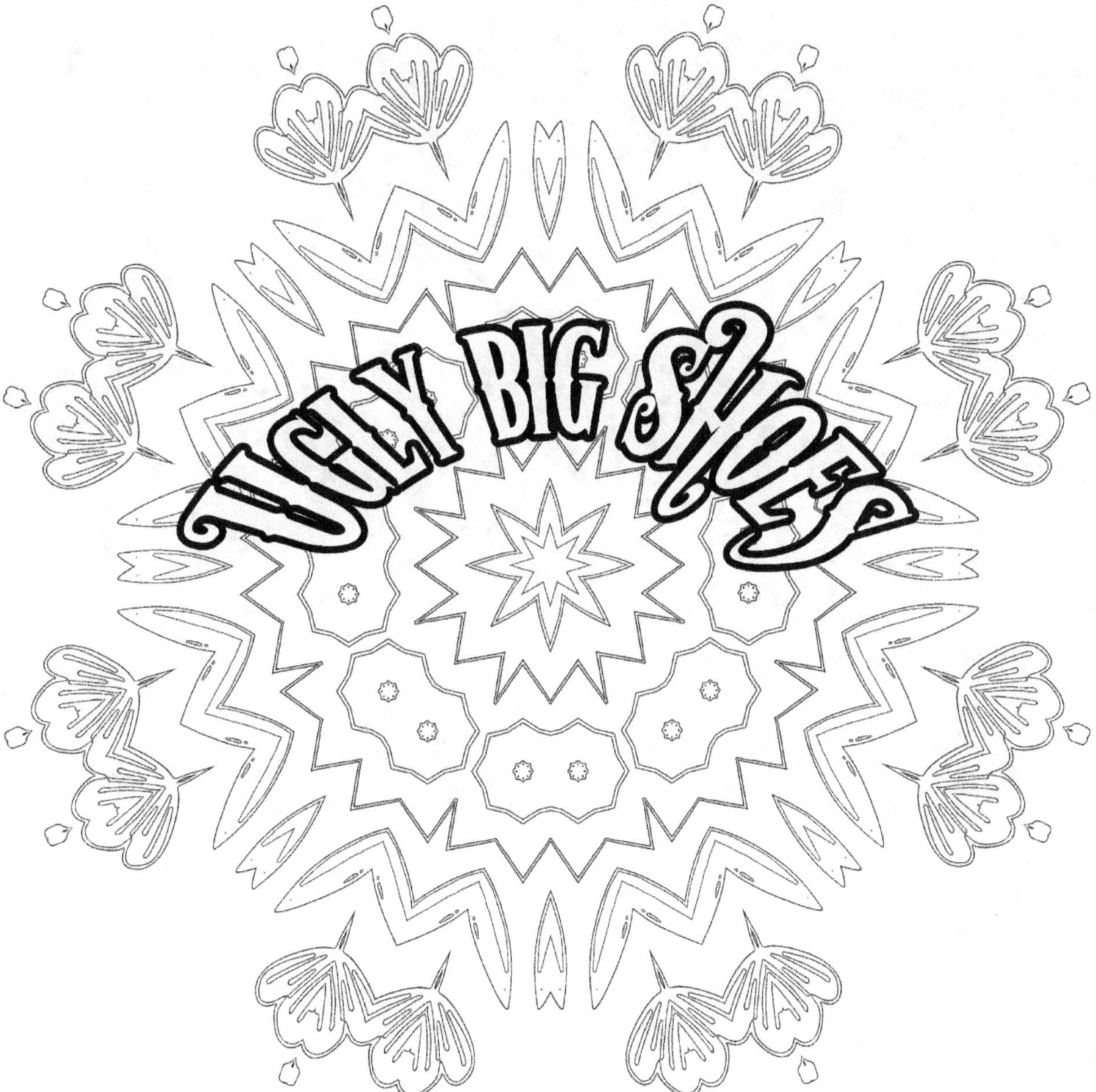
UGLY BIG SHOES

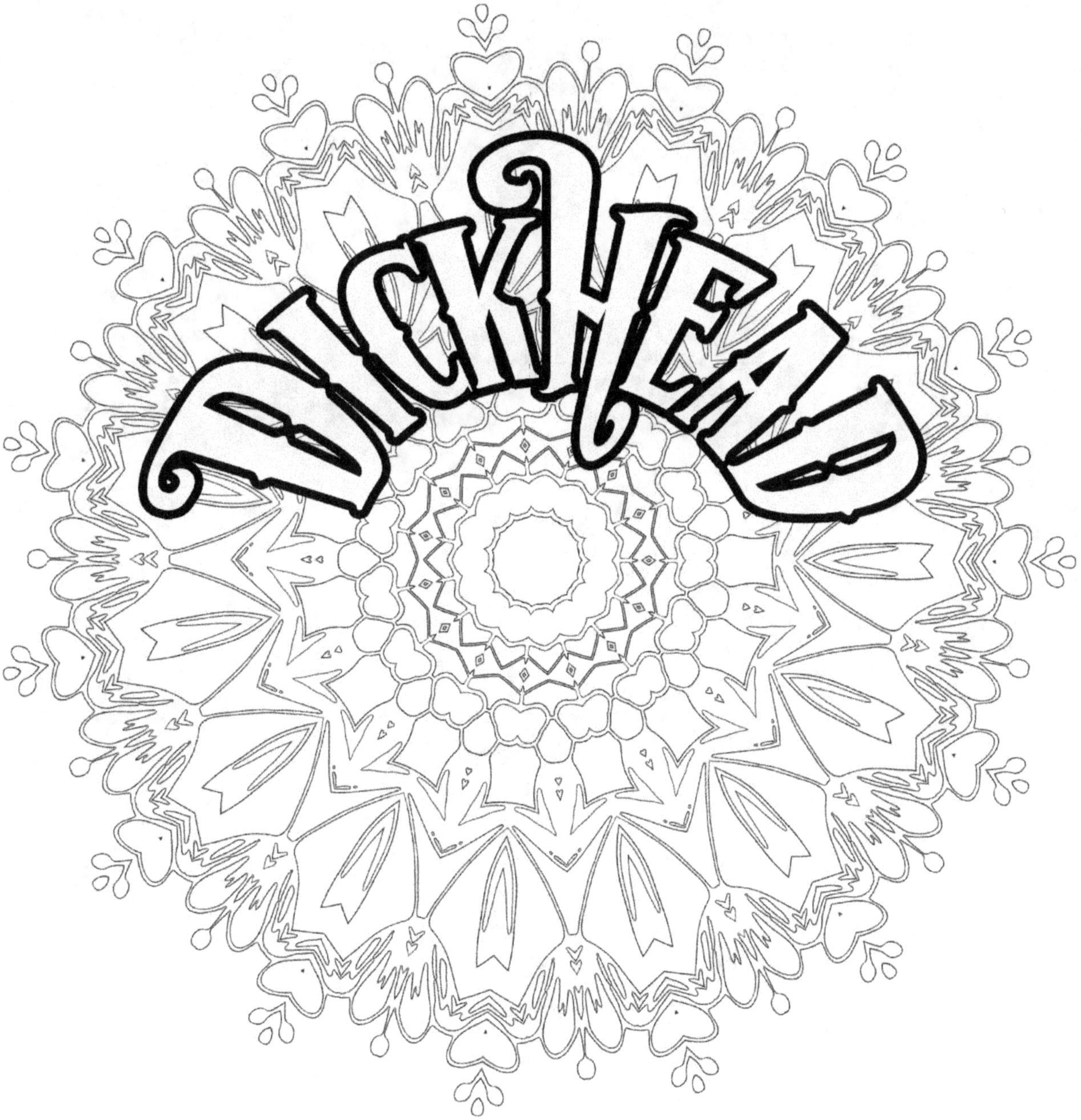
DICKHEAD

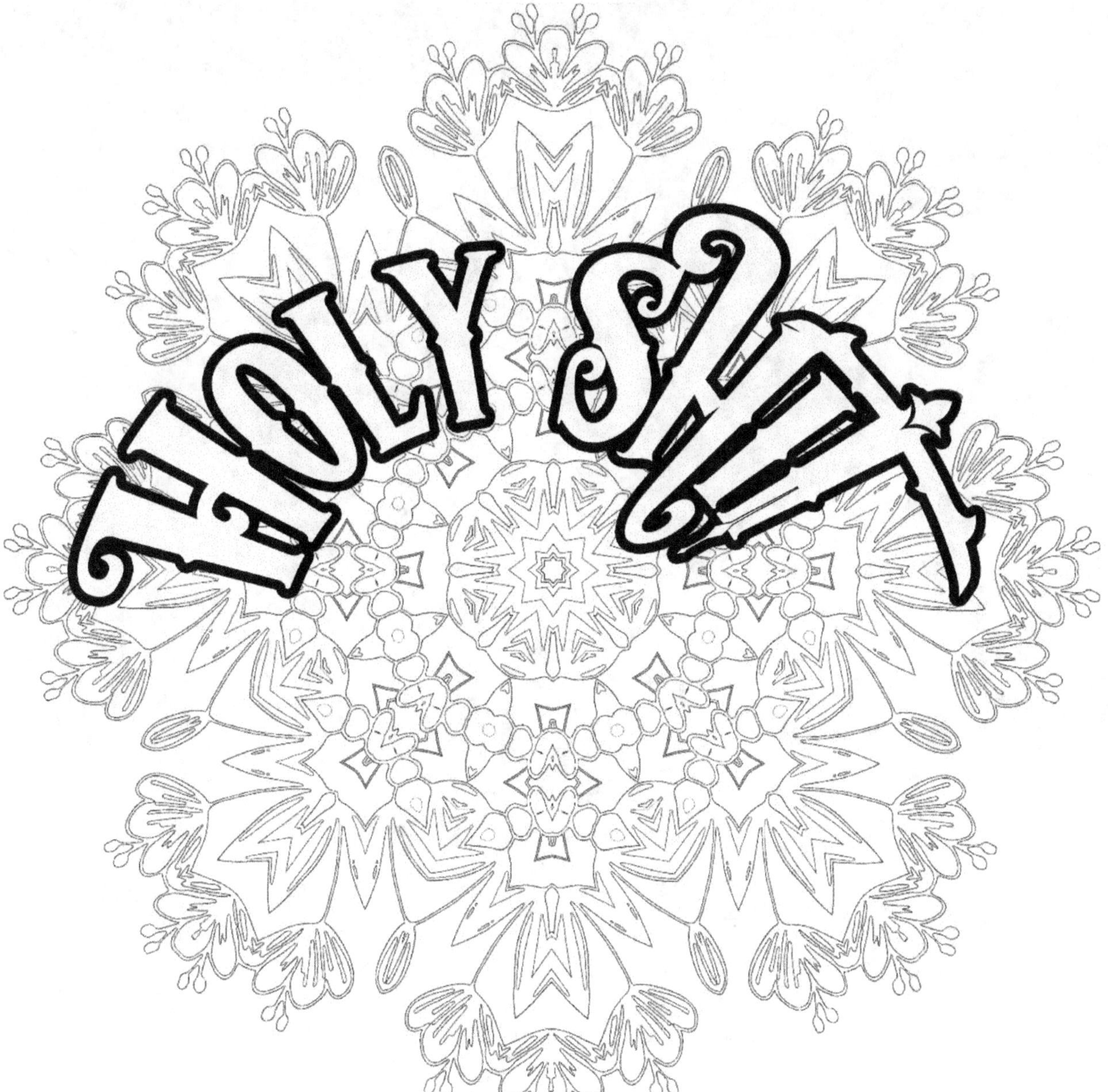
HOLY SHIT

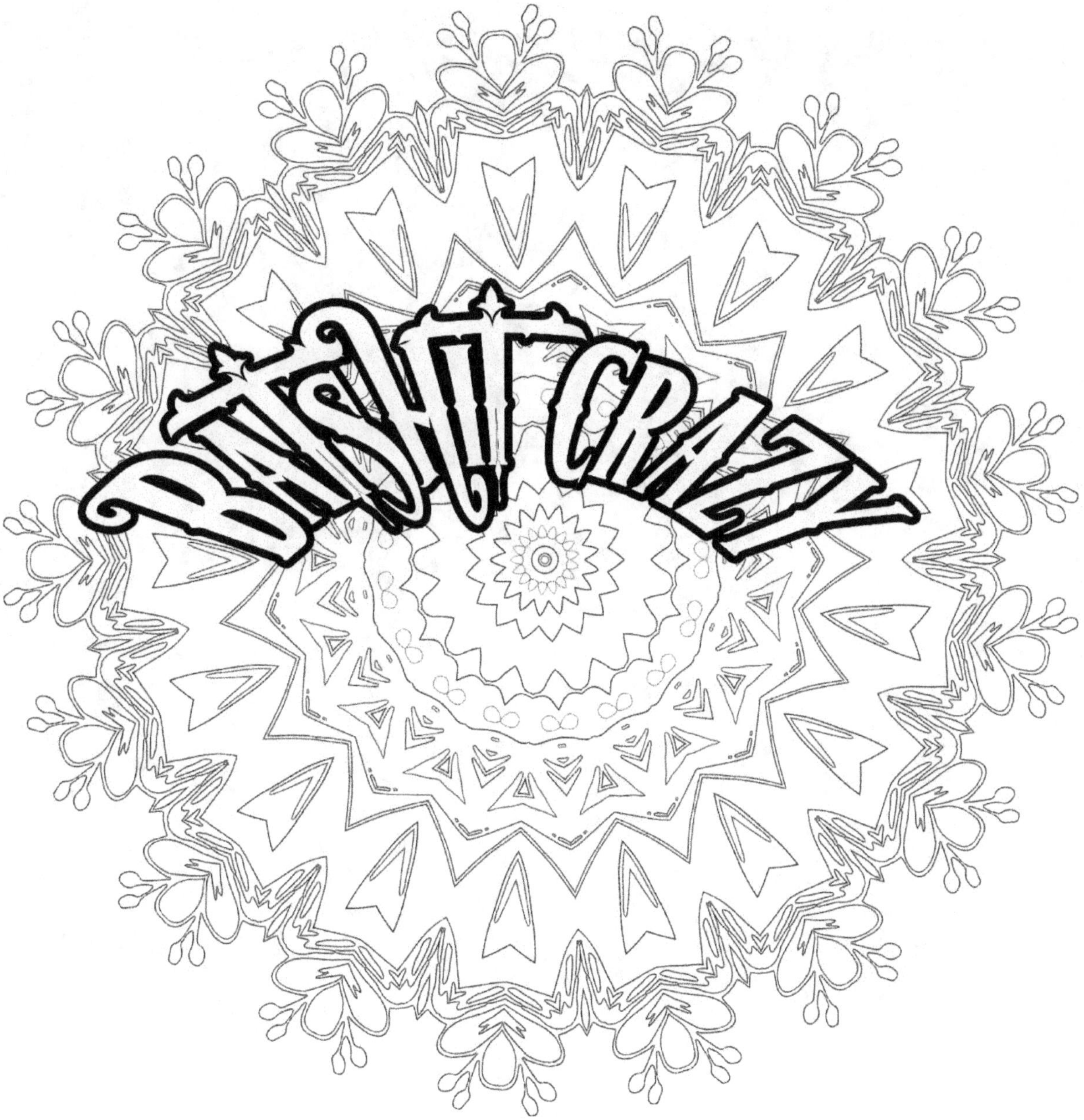
BATSHIT CRAZY

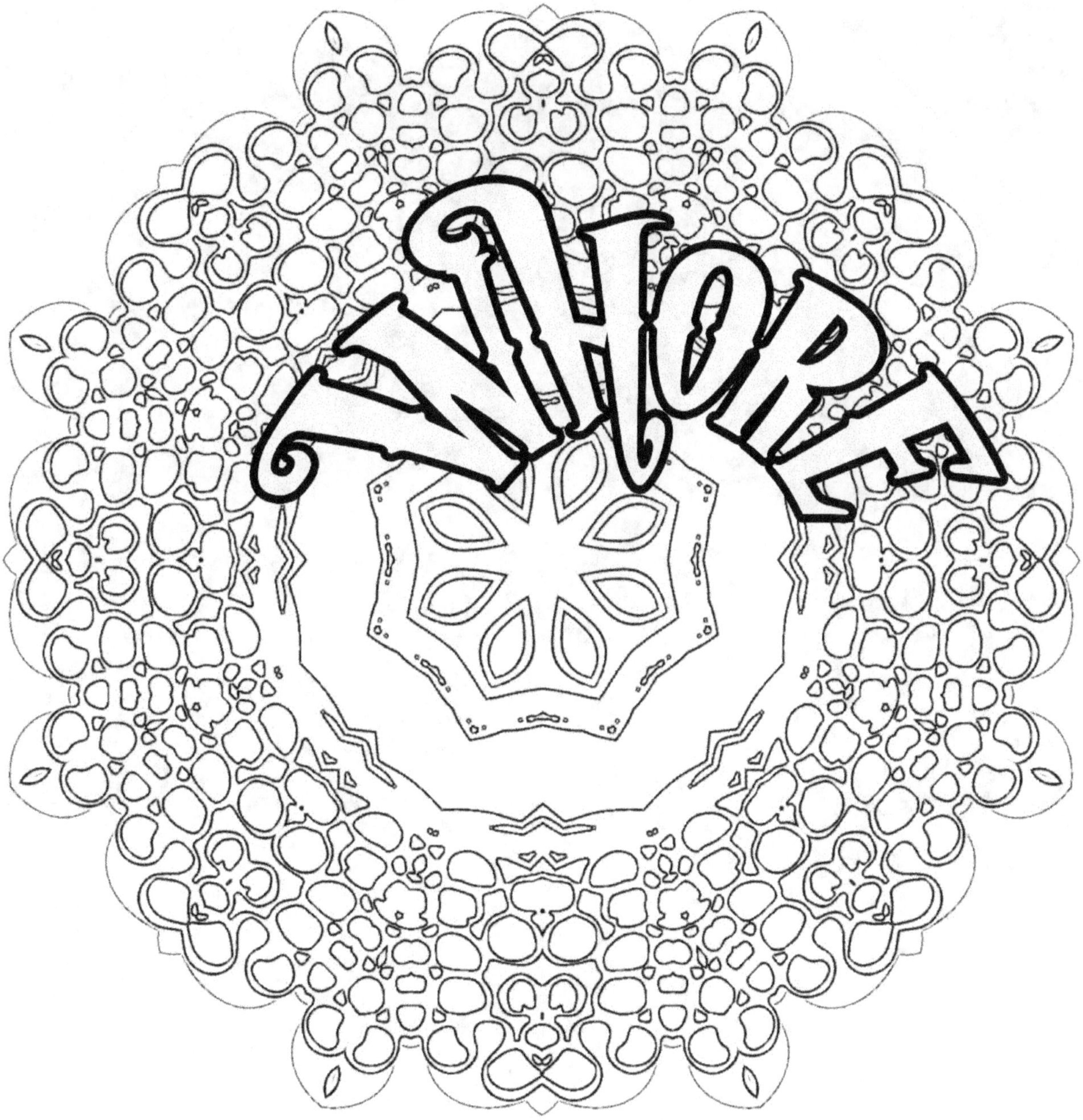
WHORE

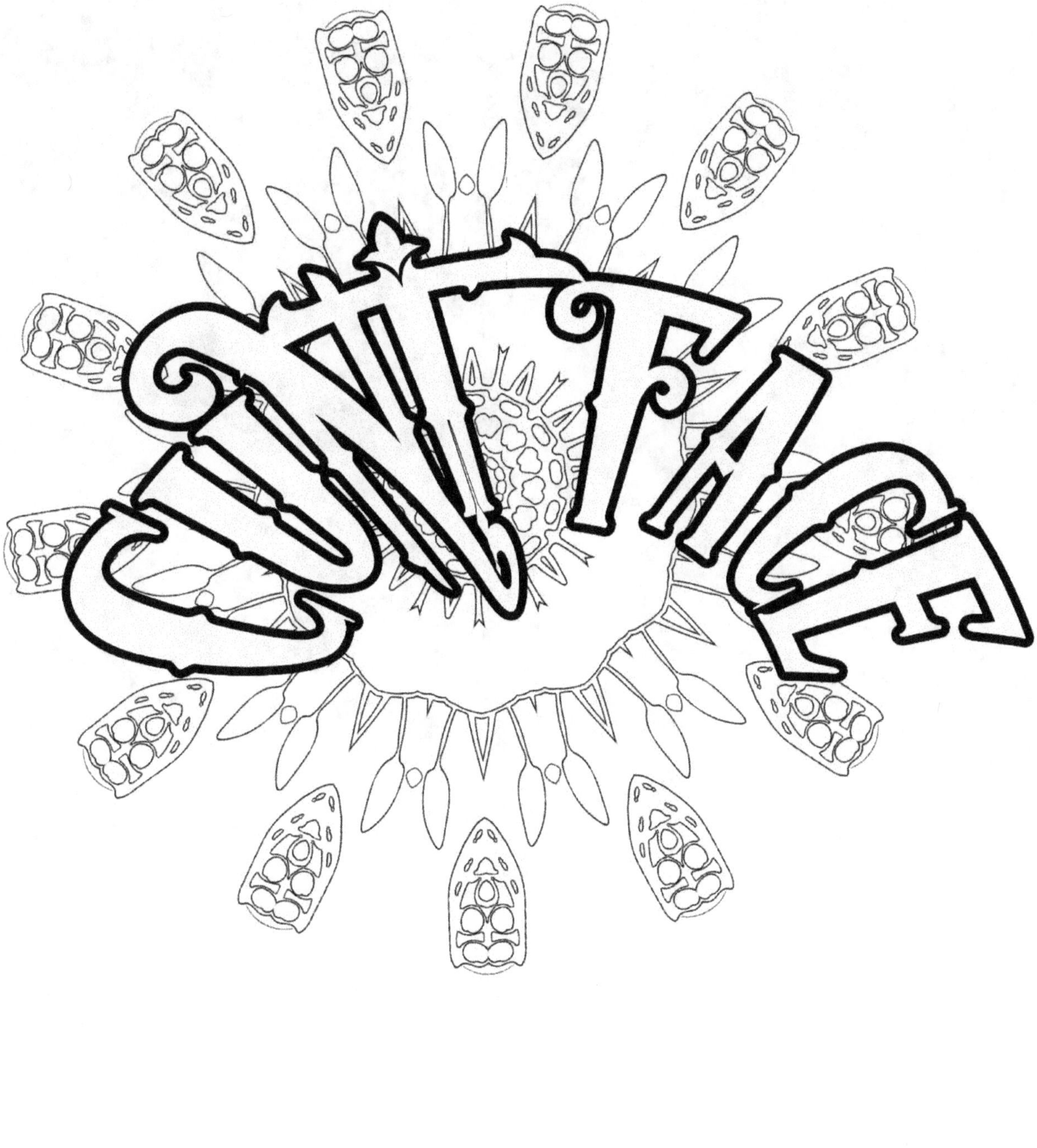
CUNTFACE

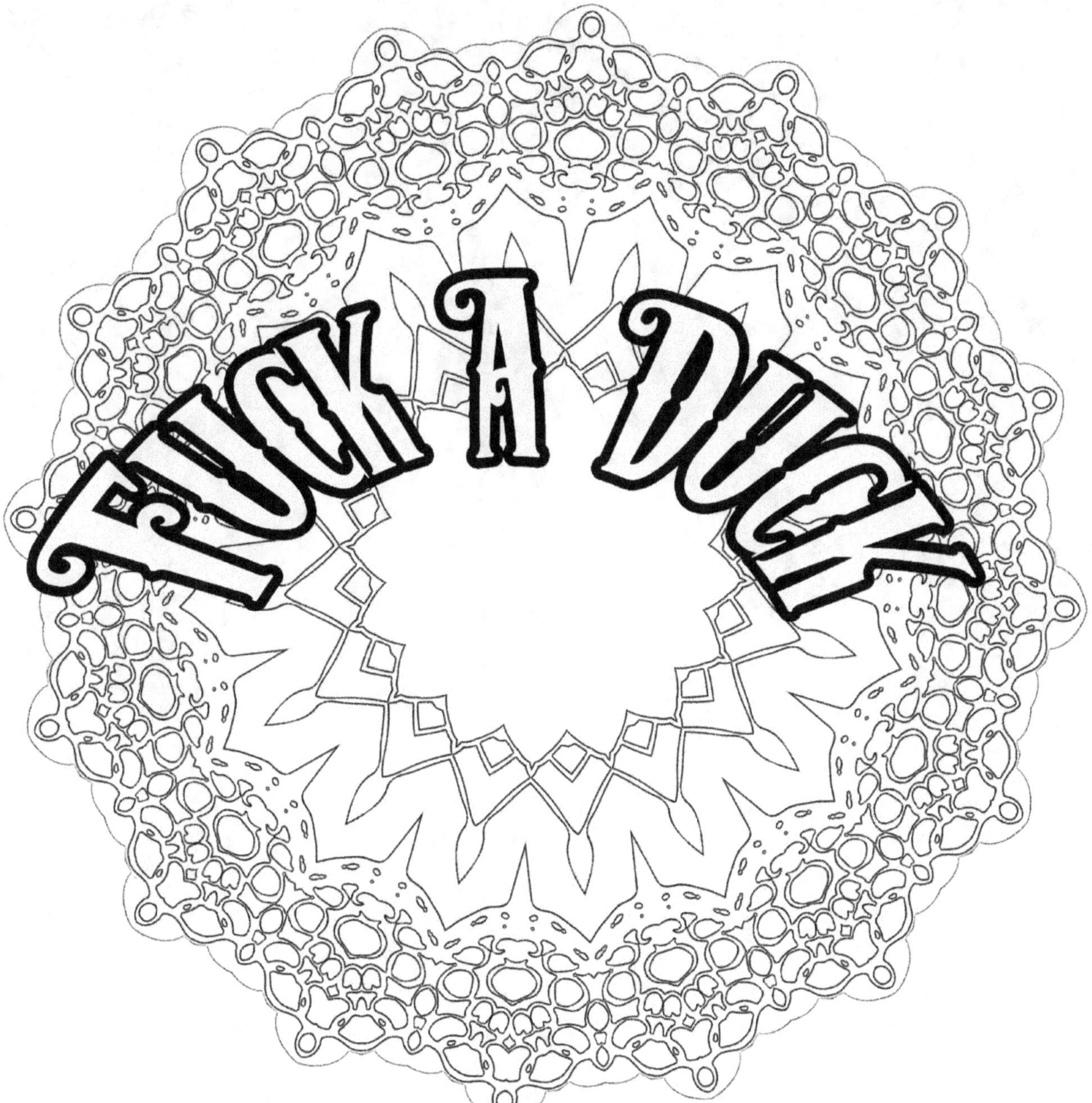
FUCK A DUCK

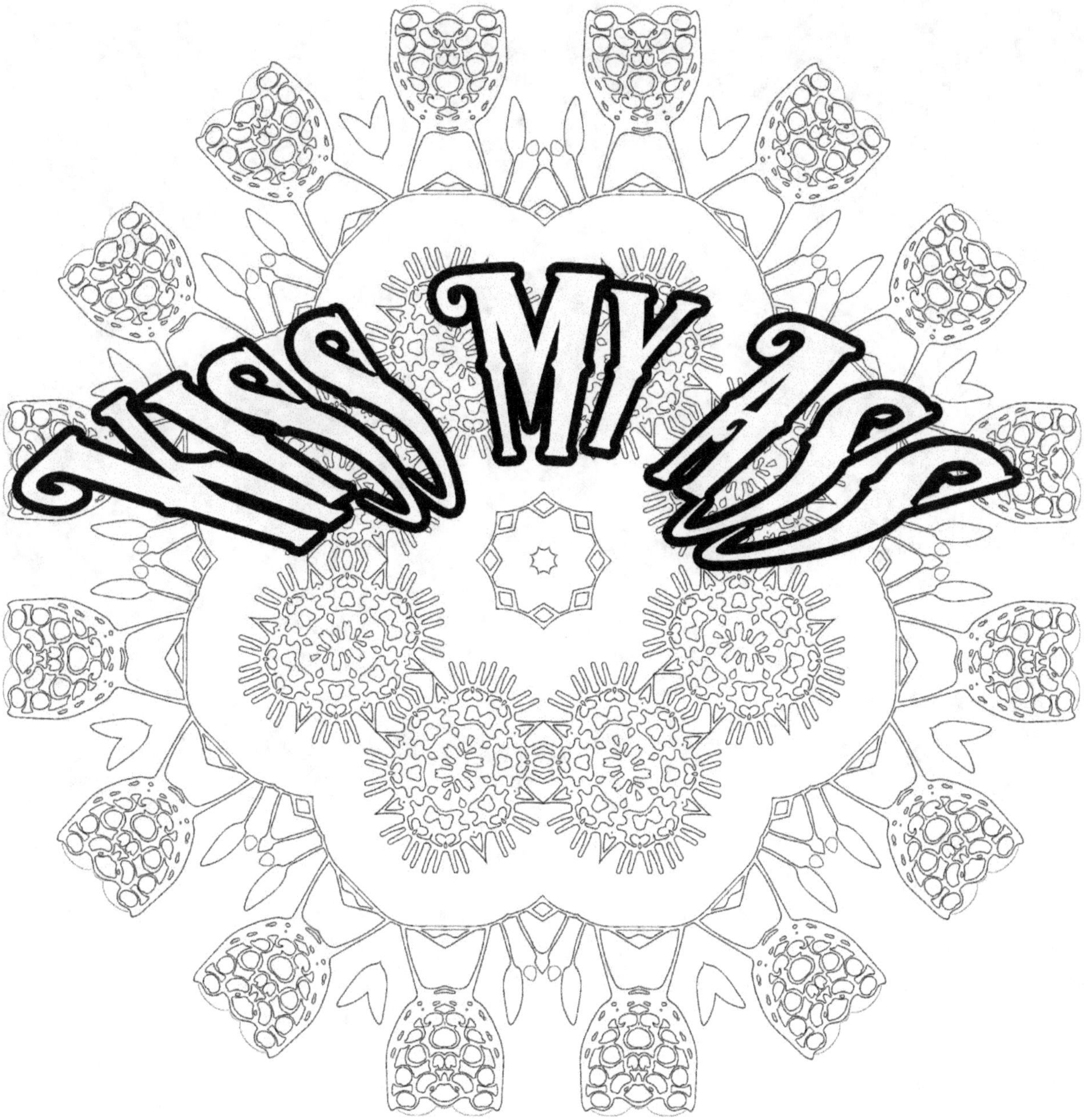
KISS MY ASS

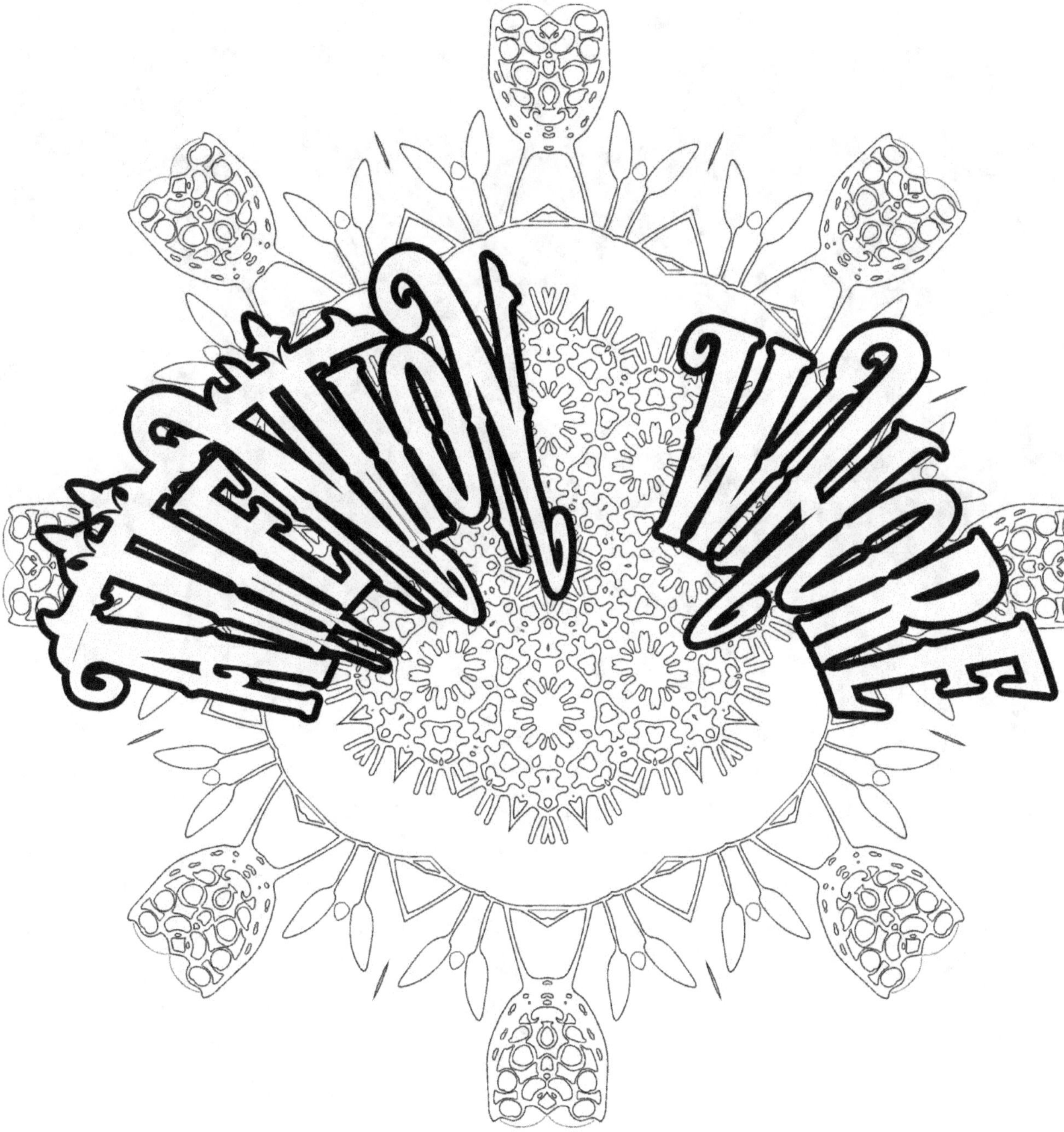
ATTENTION WHORE

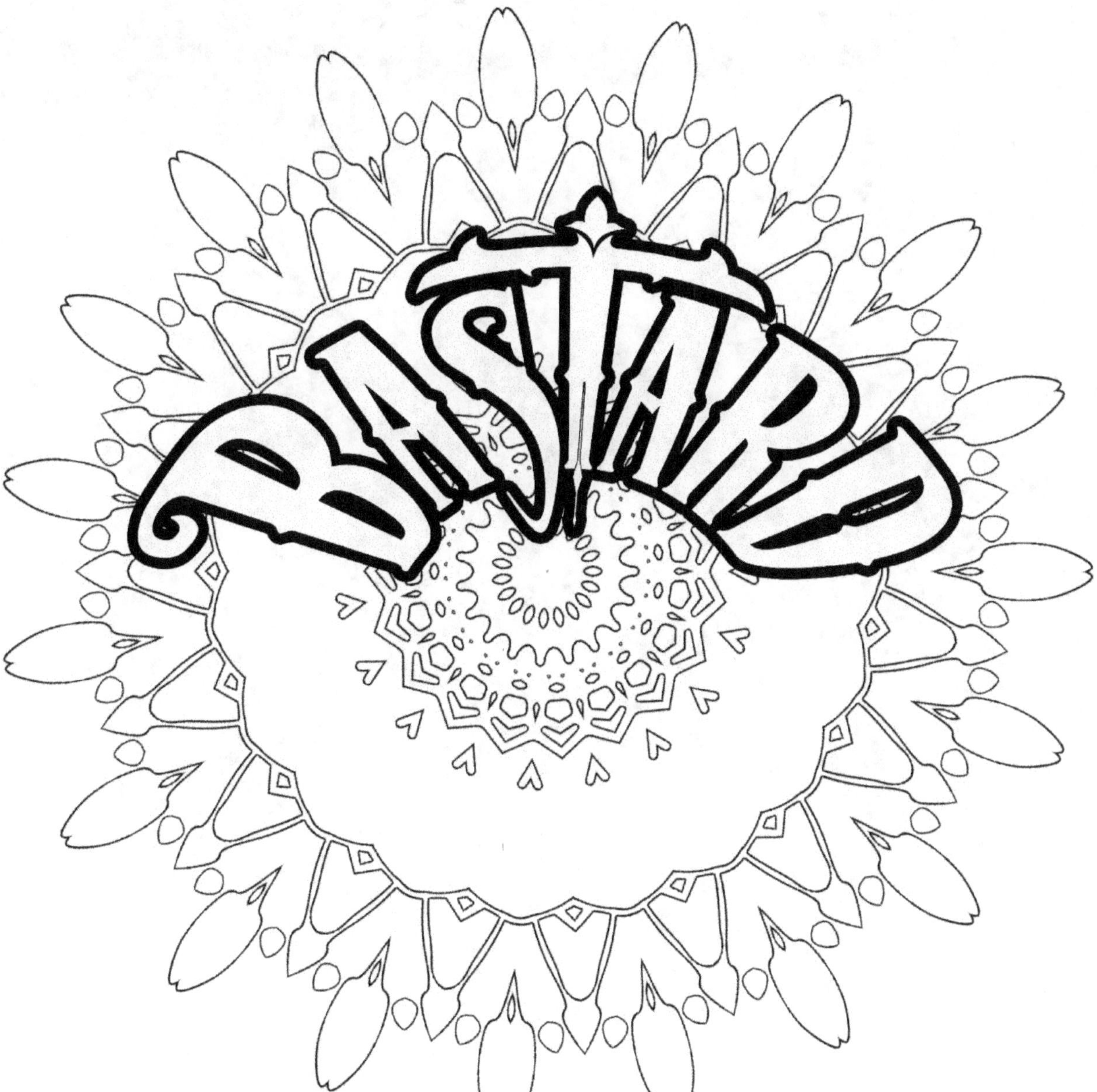
BASTARD

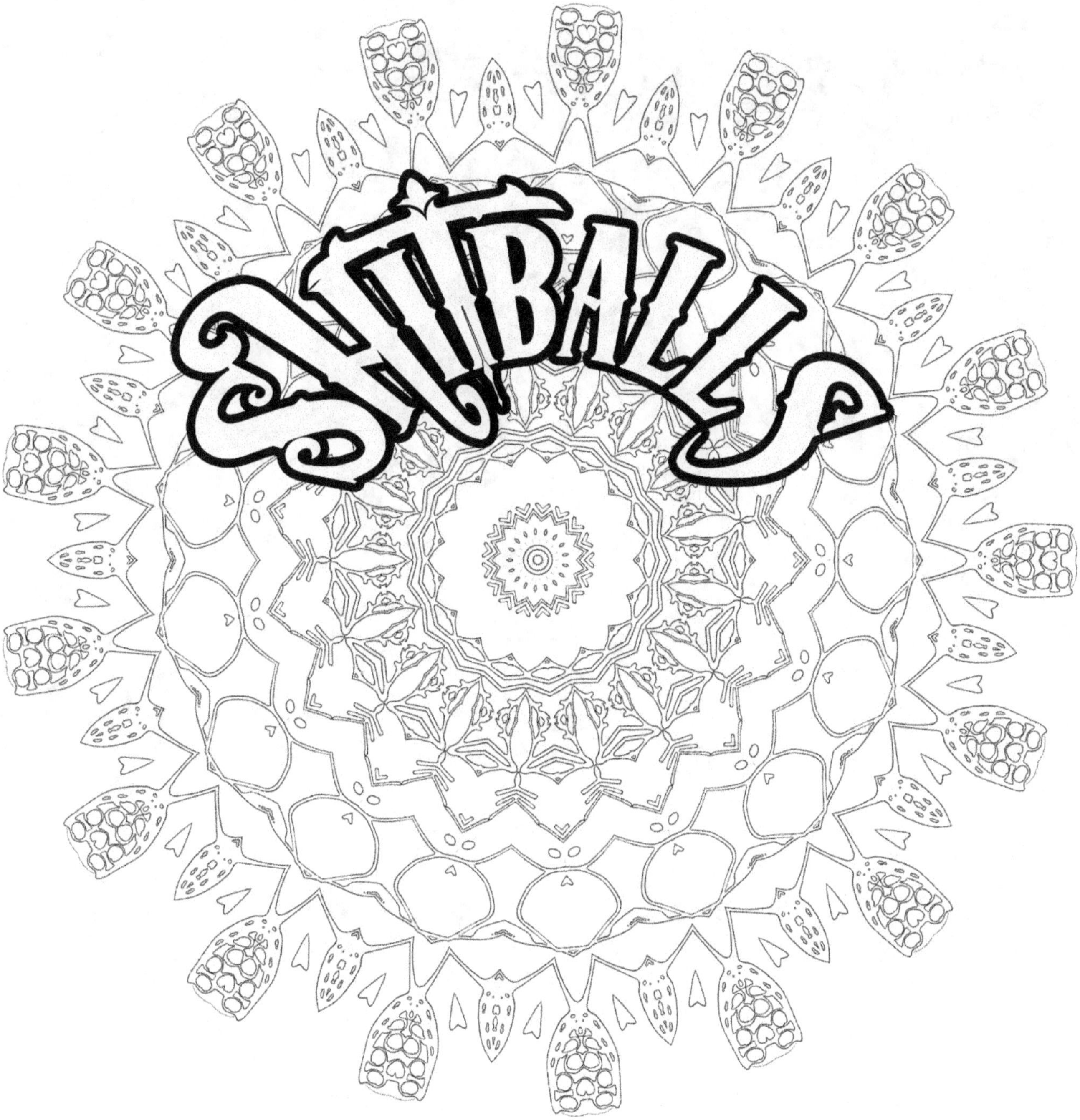
SHITBALLS

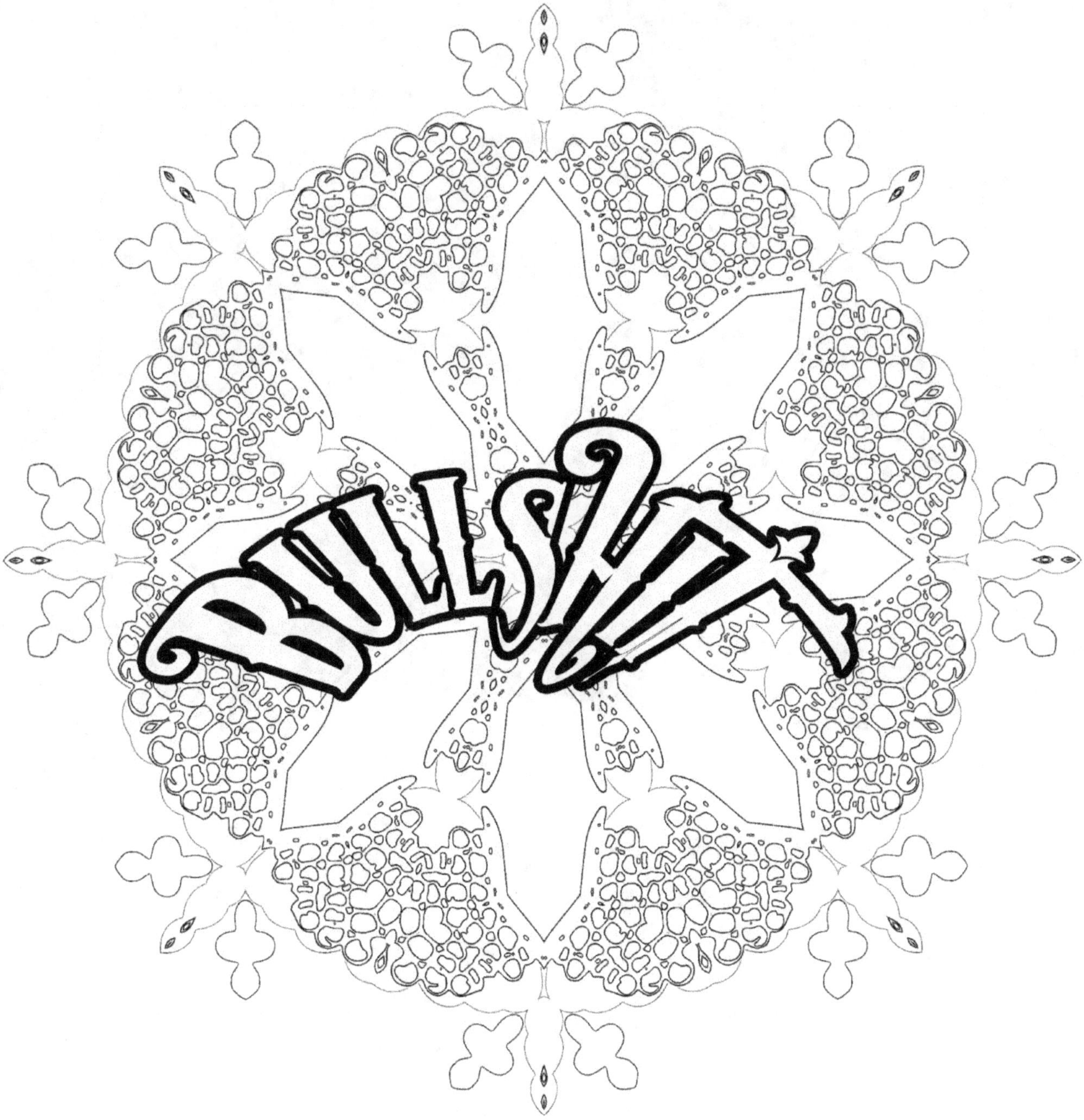
BULLSHIT

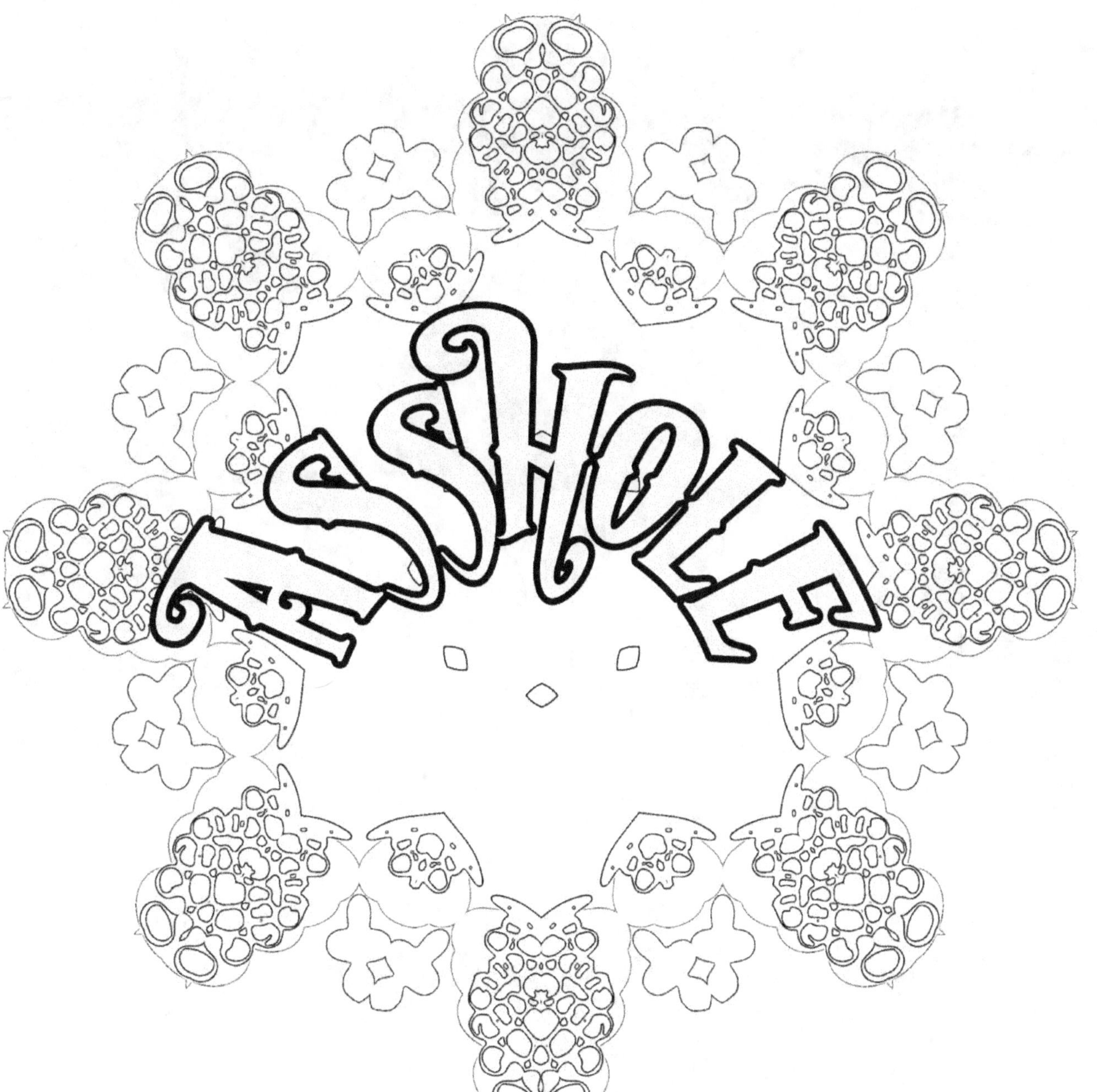
ASSHOLE

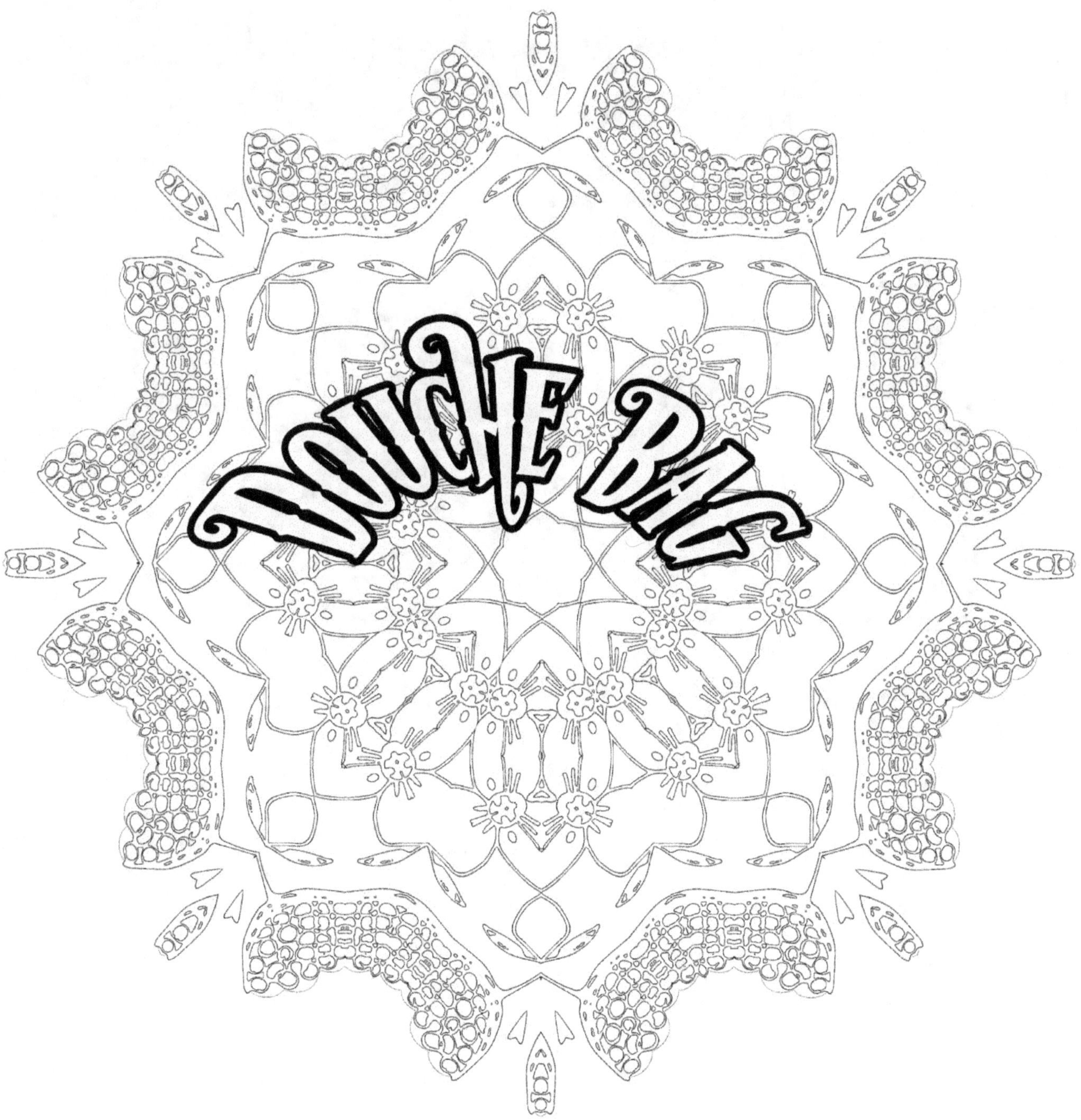
DOUCHE BAG

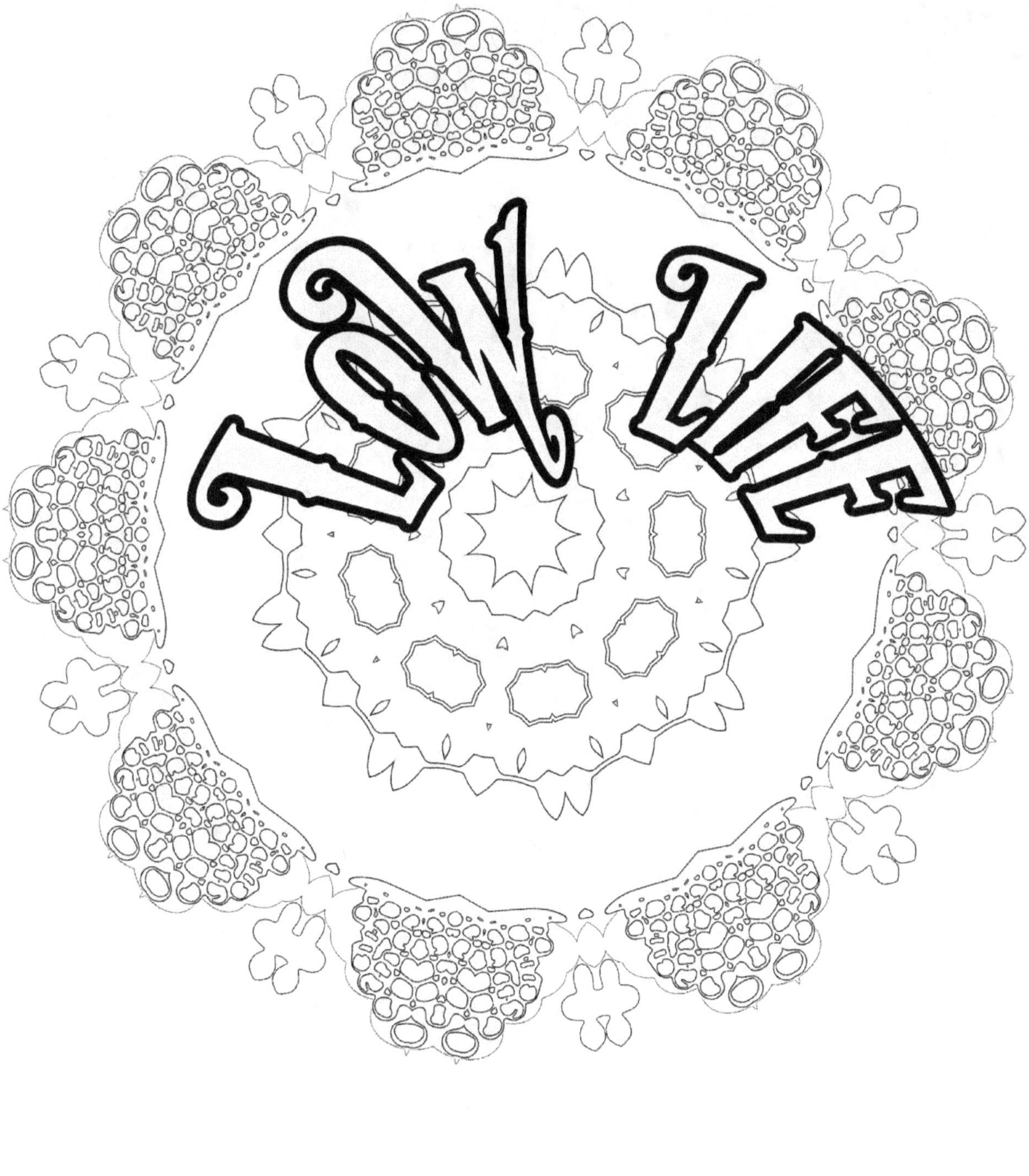
LOW LIFE

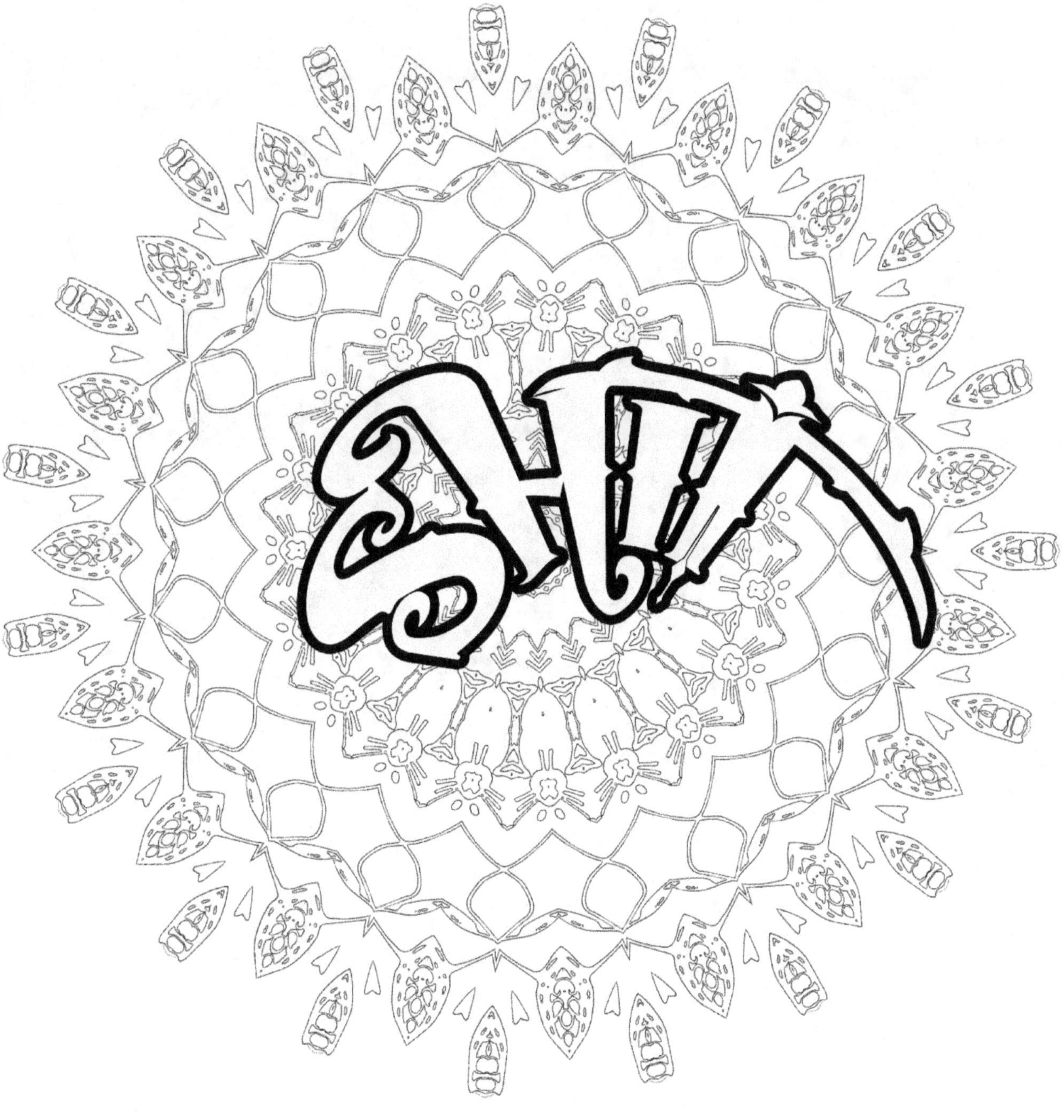
SHIT

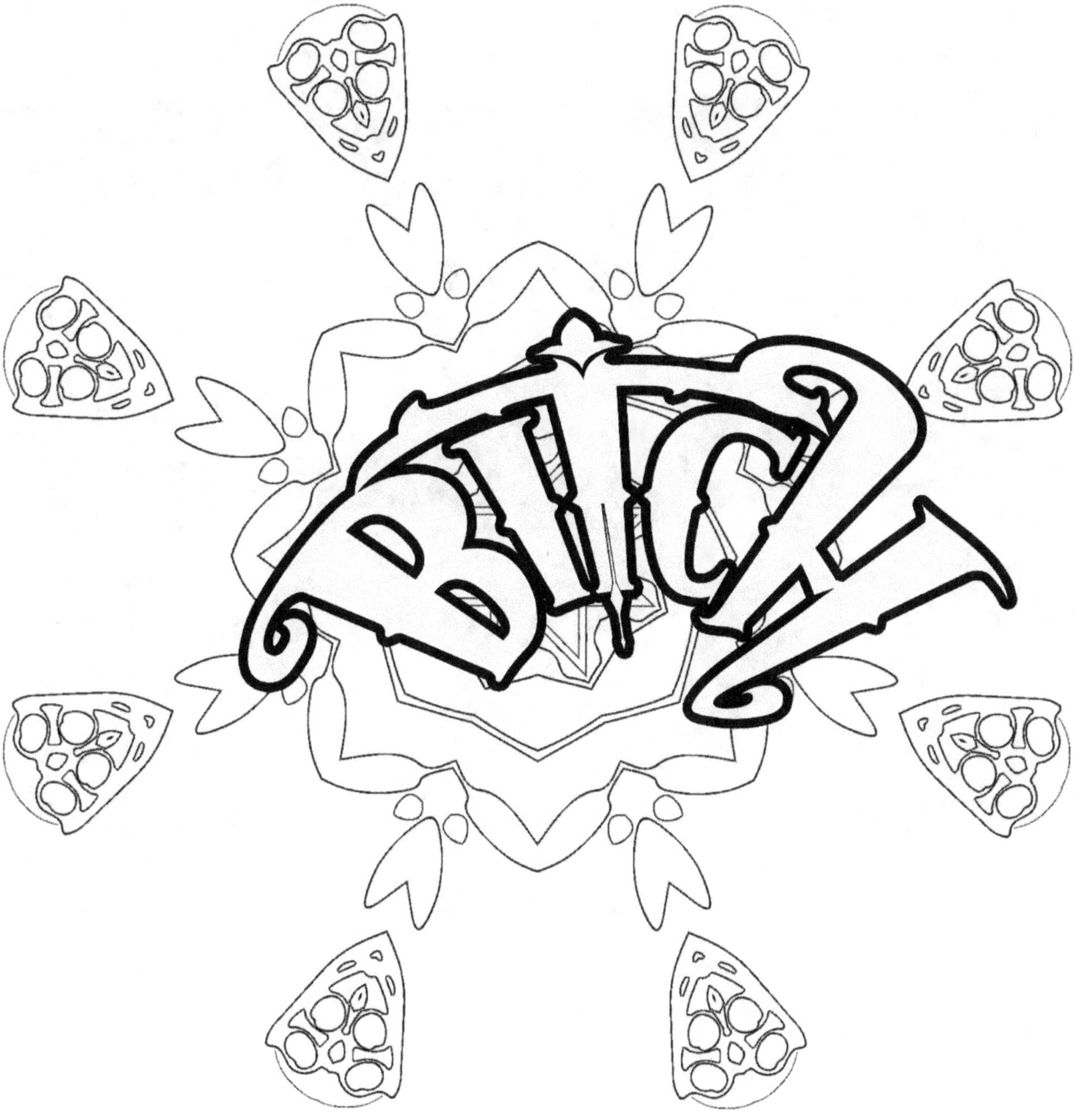
BITCH

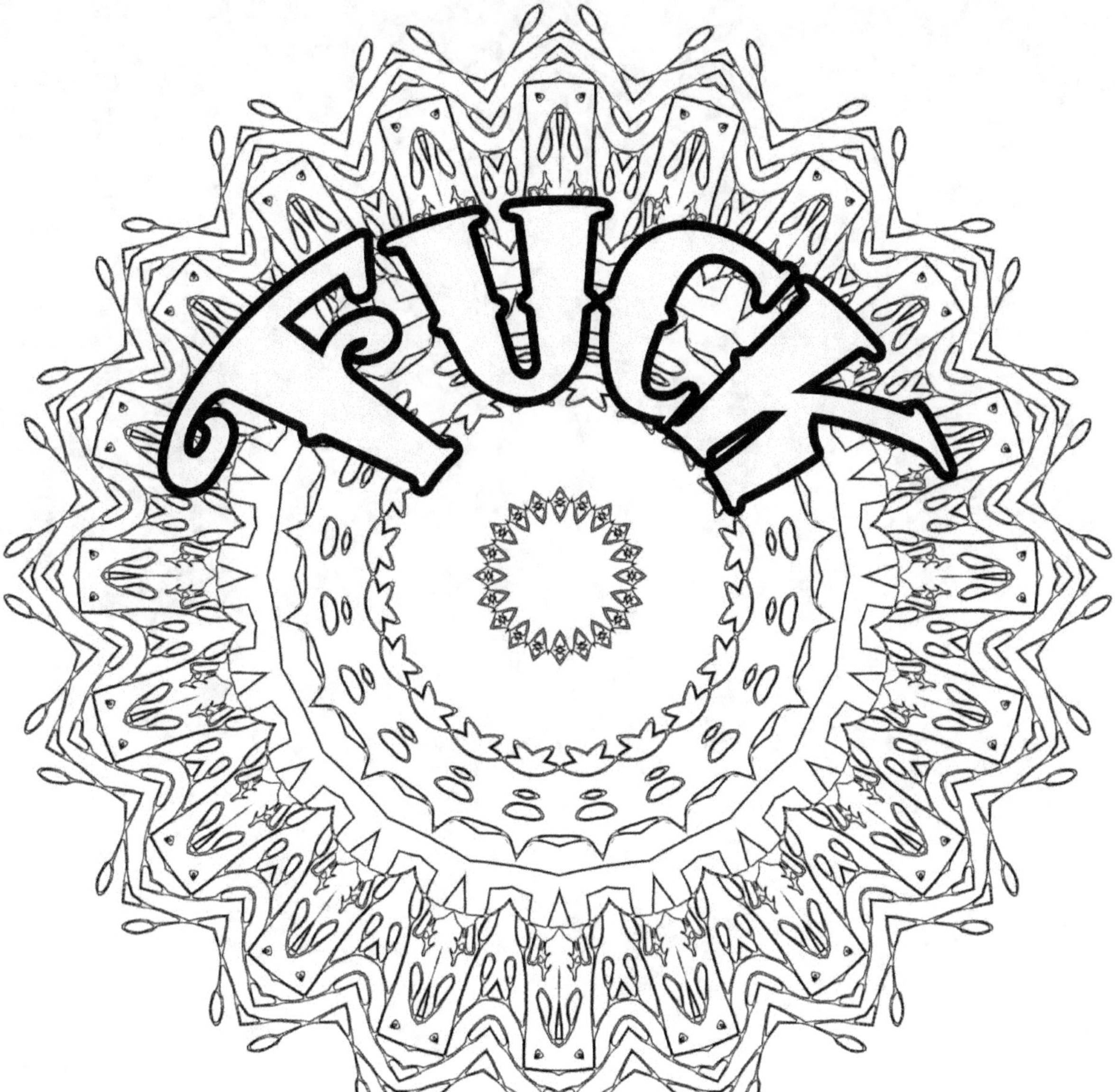
FUCK

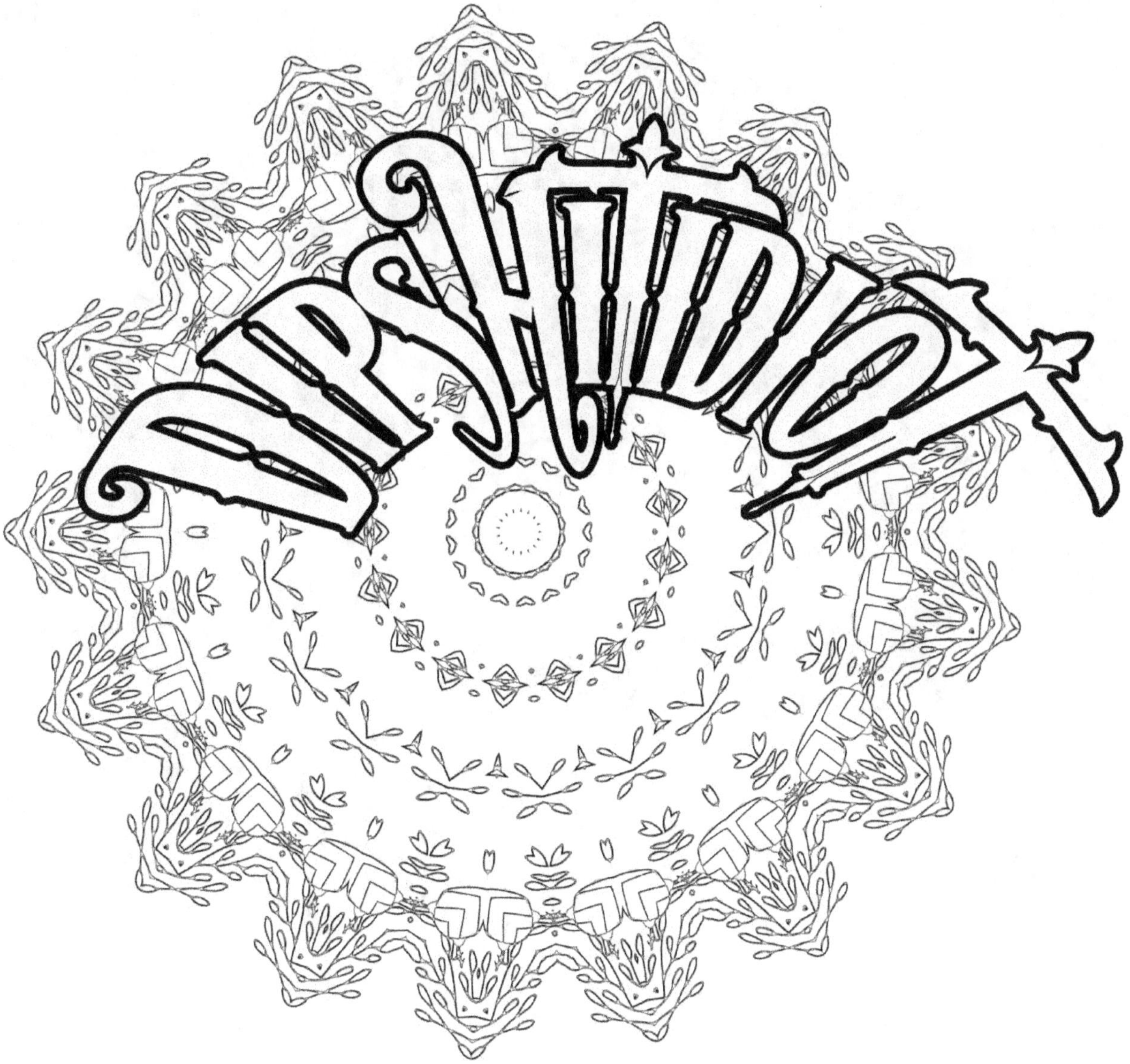

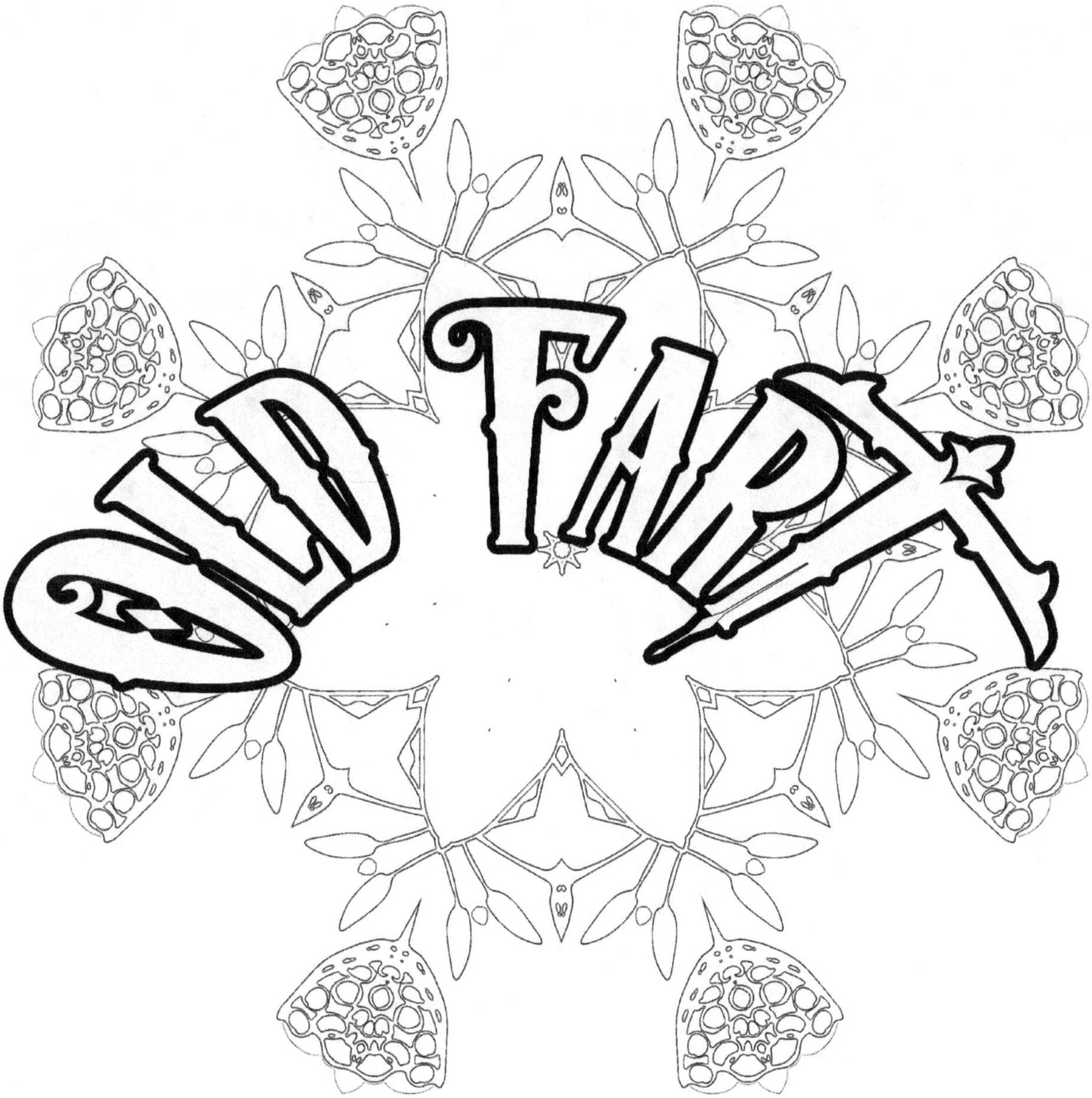
OLD FART

www.ingramcontent.com/pod-product-compliance
Lightning Source LLC
Chambersburg PA
CBHW081747170526
45167CB00009B/3948
9781544116228